# Managing the Sales Pipeline

## The Key to Consistency and Predictability in Sales

### by

I0503612

### *WW Chee*

# Books by
# WW Chee

The Sales Operations Handbook

Getting the Most Out of your CRM

Sales Operations for Small Businesses

Managing the Sales Pipeline

# Table of Contents

# Legal Notes

# Introduction

Regardless of what business or industry you are in, the stages of the sales process have more in common that most people will realize. It always starts with a lead, and is followed by engagement, then the product or service is discussed, prices are negotiated, and the deal is signed.

It may sound straightforward and simple, but each of those steps in the process can be broken down further into many steps, and each opportunity may have many variations to them. To add further complexity, individual salespeople have their own individual styles and personalities. All of these can and will affect the chances of closing a sale if not managed.

When the process is well documented, automated, and managed using best practices identified, all these variables become better managed and through the use of processes the sale becomes more predictable. When well managed, salespeople and sales managers are aware of the status of each prospect and are able to plan the sale each step of the way. This is known as pipeline management.

According to the Harvard Business Review companies with effective pipeline management showed a 15% increase in growth from companies without. Additionally, companies with three specific practices such as having a defined sales process, training management in pipeline strategies, and actually going through the pipeline review process, experienced a 28% increased revenue growth.

This book explores the sales pipeline from the perspective of sales management. I talk about the concept of a pipeline and how to manage the pipeline of the sales team to help your salespeople to move the sales forward.

This includes the setting up of a sales pipeline in your organization , to strategies you can use to build and manage a pipeline for your sales team, to metrics and performance indicators to monitor and review the pipeline. With these steps, you can develop a pipeline management practice in your organization for consistency and growth in sales.

# Chapter 1. Introduction to Pipeline Management

## What is a Sales Pipeline?

In sales, the pipeline is the sequence of actions identified as the most effective manner for a sales person to move a prospect from a lead to closing the sale. Each stage is ideally aligned to the sales process, and each stage also contains a series of tasks that the sales person needs to complete.

A sales pipeline allows management or sales operations to track the progress of each opportunity. This enables the early identification of issues and more accurate forecasting of sales.

Generally the sales pipeline can be split into four sections:

1. Lead Qualification

    The lead qualification stage is about assessing the opportunity. The sales person needs to understand the business of the prospect and his or her needs and budget for the product or service that the sales person is selling.

    Failure to properly qualify opportunities will result in wasted effort down the pipeline; either by chasing a sale that is unlikely to happen, or by taking an suboptimal approach to closing the sale.

2. Engagement

The engagement stage is about meeting the prospect and opening discussions about   the product or service that your organization is selling. This should ideally be done using     your organization's chosen sales methodology to lead the prospect to the idea that your product  or  service  is  the right choice for them.

3. Solution

The solution stage is where a solution is developed and presented to the client. Proof       of concepts are done, or a proposal is drafted along with the costs.

4. Closing

The final stage is closing the sale. This stage is where the negotiations take place and     contracts are signed.

Note that the four steps are just a general category of how a sales pipeline is organized. Individual organizations may tailor their pipeline further by breaking down a category into further, more detailed steps. There are organizations that have pipelines that contain 10 or more stages, but generally most have between 4 to 7 stages.

# The Importance of a Sales Pipeline

According to the Harvard Business Review companies with effective pipeline management showed a 15% increase in growth from companies without. Additionally, companies with three specific practices such as having a defined sales process, training management in pipeline strategies, and actually going through the pipeline review process, experienced a 28% increased revenue growth.

It is clear that the sales pipeline is an effective tool for sales people to plan and track their sales, and it is also an excellent tool for sales operations or management to identify gaps and provide support. This ensures that sales works in a consistent manner, by moving the prospects through the pipeline as quickly as possible without compromising on level of service the prospects receive from sales.

As a management tool, the sales pipeline has incredible value.

By looking at the pipeline of the entire sales organization it is easy to determine the forecast for the team by providing monthly, quarterly, half yearly, or annual projections based on the deals expected to close in that period. As the metrics are analyzed sales operations and management should have a firm grasp on the average time taken for each stage of the pipeline.

That brings us to the next benefit, which is the allocation of resources. When deals move through the pipeline at different stages, resources will be needed to facilitate the move through to the next stage. For example, if a deal is going to the negotiation stage, the finance department may be needed to provide a quotation. Or maybe the legal team needs to step in to draft a contract. When deals are being closed, marketing would need to be informed so they are able to provide more leads to feed into the pipeline again.

On the flip side, if deals are being stalled management could step in to facilitate negotiations or provide support. In some cases, a different product team might be more suited to the prospect's needs and once identified the prospect could be converted to a customer with a different approach. It is after all the manager's responsibility to identify and ease the challenges of sales people.

All this can only be done with the thorough understanding of the metrics from the sales pipeline. Having a sales process in place is essential to developing an effective pipeline for salespeople. With effective pipelines, sales operations or sales management is able to develop effective plans to manage the pipeline and provide support where needed.

## Sales Pipeline vs. Sales Process

The sales processes give a step by step stage of the sales cycle for each individual opportunity. The sales process provides a clear guide on what the sales person needs to do at each stage, what outcome to expect, and what the next stage is, from prospecting to qualifying, to close. By having a process, it reduces the time salespeople need to think about how to execute on their sales by staying consistent.

The sales pipeline should have the same stages as the sales process. However, in addition to that the sales pipeline should also contain the details of each prospect, the expected deal size, expected closing date, and other metrics.

In some organizations, the sales pipeline is presented as a spreadsheet report with each prospect or opportunity taking a row with the details in the columns

# Sales Pipeline vs. Sales Funnel

While the two terms pipeline and funnel are used interchangeably by many people, there are some subtle differences.

A sales funnel is buyer or customer oriented, and shows how prospects progress down the funnel; ultimately turning into a customer. The funnel is a visual representation of the conversion rate of prospects to customers by each stage.

A sales pipeline is seller focused and relies on a process to convert prospects, and contains actionable items for each stage. The pipeline is a visual representation of where a prospect in the sales process, and gives the sales person a guide on what to do next.

# Sales Pipeline vs. Sales Forecast

The sales pipeline and forecast gives an idea of our expectations of revenue, the focus of the forecast is the expected final revenue figure. This is used for financial projections in the business, and management tracks this against the budget.

The sales pipeline offers a clear picture of all the opportunities present, whether they may be closed or not, and it is focused on the process of moving the opportunity through the sales process. While there is an expected close date, expected close rate, and expected deal size, these are not the focus of the pipeline management process.

These metrics are used to generate a forecast for each opportunity. The sales forecast is a subset of the sales pipeline, which involves the qualified opportunities that are projected to close in a specific reporting term.

# Chapter 2: Preparing the Organization

When first implementing the sales pipeline it is important to decide on several aspects to ensure the maximum effectiveness from the pipeline.

## Understanding the Sales Process

Fig 1. The Sales Process

The sales process defines the whole selling process of a company via a journey of various stages from getting leads to closing. It is composed of activities that are required to move prospects from being a potential sale to an actual paying customers.

There is no specific definition of a sales cycle and it may vary from one business to another according to differences of business complexities. In order to be effective, a business should have a structure through common stages and every member of the sales team is aware of the stages to close a sale with recurring phases.

A well-defined sales process can bring more value to a business and can provide significant advantages for the function of the business when it comes to management and monitoring the efficiency and performance of sales.

Basically, the faster and smoother a lead converts to an actual sale, the less amount of time the client can drop out of the sale and be lost. By adhering to the sales process, the sales team can provide further analysis of the process and provide feedback to make the process better.

Furthermore, a sales process will organize the whole sales pipeline, as we will discover in the next section, because there will be a clear pipeline that is standard for all sales personnel who can easily take over any lead at any specific stage and completely aware of the requirements.

Building a structure also provides visualization, because by working on a clear image of every step, it is possible to craft an automatic response for the procedure to approach the customer and this will allow sales operations to look for a process that is effective and replicable. By improving the structure at every phase of the sales cycle, it is prudent to bring more guidance to the business by providing insights on how to direct the leads and which structures should be established to make the process more effective.

A well-established sales process will also allow the business to know its priorities. This will allow the whole sales team to save more time on every customer because they know which ones should be given more time and which one could be delegated to other members.

This enables the entire sales organization to build on a faster process that improves efficiency from top down. Identifying hot leads and filtering the non-ideal customers will allow the business to concentrate on the prospects that are easier to convert.

It is also within the responsibility of sales operations guide the business by providing a clear direction for the leads that highlight the weaker areas of the sales process. This is where the team may struggle to develop, and later on progress the prospect through the pipeline stages. This will showcase where the business is doing well in its capacity to shed light and push leads through the process.

A well-established sales process will also provide visibility and clarity of performance as well as identify areas that the sales team needs to improve. Hence, it will result to building a stronger understanding, functionality and, and solutions for the business in general.

## Align the Pipeline to the Process

There are many advantages to aligning the sales pipeline to the sales process.

Firstly, by having the same stages in the pipeline as the sales process it is easy to communicate how far along the sales cycle each opportunity is. This means that it is easy to check if the required steps have been taken, and the necessary results have qualified the opportunity to progress to the stage that it is currently at.

Visually, when the sales process and the sales pipeline are aligned it will allow sales operations and management a visual representation of sales. This allows for easy analysis of all opportunities in the pipeline.

The second advantage is that this allows sales operations and management to identify gaps through a pipeline management process. By reviewing each opportunity in the pipeline systematically, it will be evident if an opportunity is stagnant, or a deal is stalled. When this occurs, it is possible for management to deploy additional resources such as assigning a more senior salesperson to help, or provide coaching to the salesperson as necessary. Sometimes a deal may be stalled due to reasons beyond the salesperson's control, and a call can be made to drop the opportunity instead of wasting more time on the opportunity.

Lastly, by managing the pipeline with the sales process, it gives sales operations the ability to identify best practices for each stage of the process. This will ideally improve the close rates as salespeople will build a repertoire of tools or activities that can move a deal forward.

Note that the process should be developed before the pipeline as the process gives the details on each stage of the sales cycle. From there a list of actions to be taken during the stage, and the criteria needed to progress to the next stage of the sales process can be developed.

It is a practice in some organizations to use the sales process steps as the sales pipeline. This is a good practice as it avoids the confusion from learning additional terminology but sacrifices the customization of the pipeline.

## Agree on the Terminology in Your Organization

Having a consistent terminology for all salespeople, sales management, and everyone in the organization is important. This provides a consistent style and makes it easier to communicate within the sales organization.

When it is understood throughout the organization that "solution" involves developing a proof of concept and a proposal for the client and it should happen only after engaging and understanding the client's needs, it is easier for salespeople to communicate the progress of the opportunity through the pipeline. As a result, there will be more confidence in the close rates, expectations are more realistic, and when reviewing the deal there will be less time spent updating management on the progress.

## CRM and the Sales Pipeline

The best way to keep track of what's going on in the sales pipeline is the CRM (Customer relationship management) system. CRM tools and software in particular can provide a good view of the sales cycle, monitoring the progress of each lead generated. In fact, this is a common feature of most CRMs from Salesforce, to HubSpot, to Pipedrive, and many others as well.

The benefit of having up to date information available on a CRM applies to the sales pipeline as well. Using the CRM system to organize the pipeline information and keep it up to date allows for better interaction and communication in the sales organization, and between departments as well. CRM systems supplement the sales pipeline by allowing the sales teams to track their opportunities, and automate the sales process. It also allows sales operations to monitor the health of the pipeline, and manage the sales organization.

Having pipeline data in the CRM allows access to the data by sales operations. Analysis can then be done on the various metrics which makes pipeline management so much more fruitful as management can then objectively review the milestones with up to date data. Which will facilitate decision making as monthly or quarterly forecasts can be easily tracked and managed. Thereby minimizing the risk of losing a potential sale.

Opportunity Management using CRM is another crucial factor. Pipeliner, a CRM software and sales enablement company in U.S.A., has shown that the further along an opportunity is in the pipeline, the more vital it is to provide analytics. This helps to determine the priority of the opportunities, the effectiveness of the tasks, and the overall health of the pipeline in relation to the goals of the individual, the department, or the organization.

Note that the CRM should be tailored to the sales process as well as the sales pipeline that your organization chooses. Doing it the other way round will result in compromises which in the end affects the quality of the pipeline management process or lowers the efficiency of the salespeople. The CRM is a tool and it should be used to enhance the effectiveness of its users and not burden them unnecessarily with additional tasks.

If your organization is already using a CRM system, it is a good practice to regularly revisit the setup and rules of the system with regards to the sales process to ensure that the CRM system evolves along with the processes.

## Decide on the Metrics

When managing the pipeline, metrics are necessary to serve as a benchmark to measure against.

- Are enough leads being generated?
- How long should each stage of the pipeline take?
- What is the minimum deal size for a deal to be considered a priority or important customer?
- How do we weigh the priority deals, or decide on the likeliness of a close?

The short answer is that management or sometimes sales operations will decide based upon the data they have, which at the start is usually not very much. These metrics will usually be evaluated and adjusted as more data and feedback from salespeople are gathered. The important thing is that the metrics are there to support the strategy of pipeline management.

Over time as the pipeline is being used, feedback should be gathered from salespeople and adjustments can be made. Sales operations or management would also regularly review and analyze the metrics along with the sales strategy and adjustments may be made there as well. The important thing is that the pipeline metrics can and should change over time to reflect a realistic representation of how sales is performed in your organization.

For more information on the common metrics used in the sales pipeline, please refer to Chapter 5.

# Chapter 3: Pipeline Strategy

Having an organized pipeline helps in making salespeople more efficient, but it also makes managing the pipeline more effective. Developing a strategy ensures that the salespeople and the sales team at large has an organized roadmap to achieving their goals.

## Organize the Opportunities

The first step of developing a pipeline strategy is to organize the accounts. Whether by industry, revenue, or some other metric or category, having the accounts segregated into different categories allows sales operations or management to develop and fine tune a strategy for each segment.

How a salesperson would approach large corporate clients may differ from how they would handle a small business. In the case of the former, there might be a need for more presentations, stakeholder meetings, and getting buy in from executives can take time. Whereas for a small business the process might be shorter due to the accessibility of the final decision maker.

Another example would be selling to the public sector vs. the private sector, where there may be different standards of sign offs, due diligence, or compliance issues that may lengthen the sales cycle.

Yet another possibility is to sort the opportunities by the expected sales volume. By prioritizing on large accounts, sales quotas can be filled faster and the company will prioritize growth. Closing a handful of large deals may be more efficient than targeting a large number of accounts. This is especially so when there is a strain on resources.

How the accounts are organized will depend a lot on the organization, the industry, as well as the strategic plans of other departments or the entire business among other factors. Once organized, regular "housekeeping" of opportunities will ensure that salespeople will keep focus on priority accounts.

## Develop a Plan to Engage Each Opportunity

An engagement plan is an internal document aimed to provide value to the customer before the sale. This is to prepare salespeople to deal with possible questions that may arise, and arm the salespeople with the necessary information about the prospect's organization, industry, and other details.

An engagement plan should also prepare the salespeople to find information that is needed to move the opportunity forward in the pipeline. What this information is would depend on the sales methodology used. Some methodologies focus on finding key decision makers, while others try to uncover the customer's pain points in order to demonstrate value.

In my own experience, an engagement plan which collaborates with other branches or geographies of your organization is much more likely to end up successful. A prospect is more likely to move down the pipeline if you already come with case studies of how you have worked with them in other states or countries. This resulted in a 15% increased close rate for such deals.

The goal of the engagement plan is to help the customer through their buying process by providing the prospect with insights into their business or industry, and also how your organization's product or service can benefit them.

## Prepare for the Engaging the Prospect

As the engagement plan is an internal document, the external material needs to be prepared. This includes tailoring presentations and other materials to each prospect, and preparing responses for the more common questions. If your organization has a sales operations or sales enablement function, they should be the ones managing these resources.

A consolidated resource of presentations, templates, case studies, and other material can not only save time and ensure a standard of professionalism when facing the prospect.

# Get Sign-off from Internal Stakeholders

Once the material is ready, it is good practice to meet with internal stakeholders and go over the engagement plan and the materials for the prospect. Remember that the purpose of sales processes, which the pipeline is based on, is consistency. However this is also balanced by feedback from salespeople and can evolved when best practices are uncovered.

Meeting with internal stakeholders is important to not only review the plan and materials and ensure that it aligns with the prospect's buying process, discussing a deal with internal stakeholders provides access to experienced personnel who may offer additional insight that a salesperson handling the opportunity might overlook.

This is especially important with larger, high value opportunities.

# Chapter 4: Tracking Opportunities & Forecasting

Managing the sales pipeline is all about tracking opportunities. The main purpose of this is to manage these opportunities and share information about the pipeline with the organization. Understanding how individual opportunities are progressing can be interpreted for different insights in different departments.

## A Realistic View of the Pipeline

Before we look at tracking the opportunities and forecasting the sales, there are three important fields of information in the pipeline. These are not performance indicators, but fields that are either calculated or entered by the salesperson assigned to the prospect to give a more realistic view of the pipeline.

However, these fields tend to the subjective side and are estimates and forecasts. They are a best guess of how things will turn out and therefore relies a fair bit on the gut feel of the salespeople. These should be taken with a grain of salt.

### Weighting of Opportunities

A weight of each opportunity is the likelihood of closing the sale. In some organizations, the weight of each opportunity may be used to determine the percentage of the deal value to be expected or is assigned by salespeople as their gut feel on how likely the client is expected to sign on the deal.

Another way of weighting opportunities is to assign a fixed value to each stage of the sales process. This is usually not uniformly assigned; a 5 stage sales process does not automatically mean that a deal will have an additional 20% chance of closing with each stage.

Instead, the flow rate is used to determine the percentage chance of a deal moving through to the next stage. Such data should be regularly updated to reflect the changes in the organization as the process is refined or the salesperson's skill and experience increases.

### Assigning a Deal Value

The deal value is the salesperson's estimation of how much the prospect is expected to spend. This field of information is mainly used for calculating forecasts and the probability of deals being closed.

This is also used for assigning opportunities as you would want the most experienced salespeople leading the engagement on the largest opportunities.

### Expected Close Date

Expected close date as implied, shows when the deal is expected to close. By calculating the sales cycle of previous deals that were closed it is possible to estimate the close dates of new opportunities.

# Tracking Individual Opportunities

Since there have been sales pipelines it has been common practice to use tools such as a CRM system or even Excel spreadsheets to track opportunities.

Understanding where opportunities come from, and how they are progressing through the stages of the sales pipeline will give insight to sales operations or management. This can then be used to figure out what salespeople need to do in order to progress the sale and ultimately close the deal.

This might be as simple as getting the salesperson assigned to the opportunity to schedule a follow up call, or keeping the customers updated on recent developments via email. Keeping the prospect engaged ensures that the opportunity does not turn cold where it could be prevented.

## Coverage of Accounts in Pipeline

On a more strategic level, tracking opportunities in the pipeline is a useful tool for sales operations and sales management. This allows decision makers a view on the number of opportunities at each of the stages of the pipeline, along with the deal values and how they move along the pipeline.

This is invaluable as decisions can then be made on how to prioritize the opportunities and allocate resources to each of them. Whether this is to focus on larger deals or to keep opportunities from going stale, action cannot be taken without the information provided by the sales pipeline.

Attention should also be paid to how deals entering the pipeline are being developed. It is common for salespeople to be focused on chasing a deal, and very often opportunities at the later stages get more attention than the new leads. This situation is less than ideal as new leads are what keeps the sales pipeline flowing, ensuring future wins. Having a sales pipeline management strategy that includes this is important to keep a healthy pipeline.

A strategic view of the pipeline also allows sales operations to identify bottlenecks in the sales process. For example, if there is a lack of support in the legal department then deals will be stuck when they hit the stage when contracts are negotiated. Identifying these issues will allow additional headcount to be hired in this example, or client expectations can be managed better on the timeline.

## Monitor Results vs. Target

Understanding the total deal value in the pipeline at each stage allows better forecasting of sales. It is important to ensure that the pipeline has sufficient deal volume to be worked on so that the targets can be met.

Additionally, if the metrics of the pipeline are well managed it will be possible to determine the deal velocity and the win rates. This will give a more accurate number on the sales in each period.

Action can then be taken if these numbers are projected to fall short instead of being caught by surprise just before the end of the period.

# Chapter 5: Pipeline Metrics

When dealing with the sales pipeline, there are a number of metrics that will help you measure the health of the pipeline and manage the opportunities. These metrics can help sales operations to manage the sales process and create effective benchmarks and tools for the sales team. This makes it much easier to project the future success of the sales team. When employing performance indexes, it is possible to achieve forecast precision within a 5% margin of accuracy.

This means that sales managers will be able to know not only how the team is performing at the present, but be aware of possible issues that may arise in the future and take early preventive actions..

## Monitoring by Segments

Forecasting is just the tip of the iceberg. Using the expected close dates, with the deal volume, and weighting of the opportunities as described earlier in Chapter 4 it is possible to get an accurate forecast of sales. However, there is a lot more insights that can be gleamed from analyzing the pipeline.

When organizing the pipeline into channels, sectors, or segments it opens up the possibility of analyzing the pipeline by these categories. Reviewing the accounts in each of these segments tells us how each segment is performing relative to the others. It also shows us how well the prospects in each segment is performing, and how well the salespeople are performing.

The sales volume from each segment will also be another metric to pay attention to, as well as the average sales volume per prospect in each segment. A higher volume in a segment shows more high value prospects where the effort from salespeople will yield higher returns. Also, comparing each opportunity against the average sales volume per prospect will show how much priority should be placed on the opportunity.

The cost of sales and average cost of sales per prospect in each segment is another metric that should be watched. A longer sales cycle or the need to commit more resources is a consideration when deciding how viable each opportunity is. This should be balanced with the average sales volume for management to make the decision on which opportunities to prioritize.

## Monitoring Pipeline Health

In addition to the above, there are additional metrics to monitor the health of the pipeline. A healthy pipeline ensures that salespeople have enough opportunities to work towards their sales targets, and that they are progressing the opportunities well towards closing the deal. Therefore each of these metrics monitor an aspect of the pipeline, and gives insight on a possible weakness in pipeline management.

**New Leads by Source (Monthly)**

Tracking the leads by source gives insight into the effectiveness of each source. As leads are people or businesses who are interested in your organization's product or service, generating leads and converting them is crucial to the long term success of your business.

By tracking and managing the leads by source it allows you to focus on the right leads by understanding what works for your organization. Tracking new leads by source also allows the organization to understand how well its lead generating activities are performing. Also, it helps to know where most of the leads come from or how new marketing initiatives are doing. For more information about lead generation, see Chapter 6.

**Progression by Pipeline Stage (%)**

As a prospect moves through each stage of the pipeline, they have invested more and more time with your organization and have had more interactions with your salespeople. Understanding the percentage of opportunities that progress from one stage to another can show gaps in the pipeline, and may be a potential areas that can be optimized. This metric is usually calculated by number of opportunities (by number, not sales volume) for a specified time period; e.g. by month or perhaps by quarter.

Commonly there will be a stage where the progression percentage will increase. Once a prospect crosses to a certain stage they are more likely to commit to a solution. This will help in identifying the actions necessary to solidify the prospect as an eventual customer, thereby strengthening and evolving the sales process.

Prospects that drop out of the pipeline are known as "leaks". Understanding why these leakages in the pipeline occur will help to close the gap by developing alternatives to plug the leaks, or developing an alternative solution such as a more budget or value offering tailored to these prospects.

Sometimes the leak happens due to issues on the prospect's side such as a lack of budget, or they may not be sure of the solution or product that they are looking for. In these cases it is beneficial to identify these prospects early and drop them from the sales pipeline to focus on prospects that will more likely close.

**Conversion of Leads to Close (%)**

This metric tracks the percentage of the number of leads (not by sales volume) that eventually turn into closed deals. This includes deals that are closed because they are lost, or dropped out of the pipeline, as well as deals that are won. As a result this number is expected to be different from the win rate.

This metric shows the number of opportunities that the sales person or sales team have worked on till completion. This metric is usually an indication of the quality of leads.

**Win Rate**

The win rate is the percentage of opportunities closed that were wins. This is the metric that management focuses on most often, as it shows the success of the sales team. In conjunction with the other metrics, it can give insight onto which source of leads are working better than others, or which segment of prospects are more likely to close a deal.

Tracking the win rate over time may also reveal a gap if there are inconsistencies in the win rate. If there are huge variations in the win rate by quarter or month and it is not due to seasonal variation, it may be a red flag and should be investigated.

Increasing the win rate is the focus of sales operations and sales management, and this is usually achieved through developing strategies, training, coaching, and other kinds of support. However, while this metric is the bottom line of sales it should not be the be all and end all when managing the pipeline.

**Average Opportunity Size**

A large win may be a cause for celebration, and it is logical to assume that a large opportunity will be the first step to that goal. However, the larger the opportunity is the more likely it will progresses along the pipeline more slowly and require more attention and support from the sales team.

Understanding the average size of the opportunities allows sales operations to flag when an anomaly appears in the pipeline. Qualifying these large opportunities are crucial as very commonly it may be an error in the system, or perhaps a prospect may be just fishing for quotations.

**Average Size of Wins**

The average size of wins shows the sweet spot of the organization's sales team. This is where the sales team is performing at their most effective. This helps in identifying future opportunities where a win is more likely.

Comparing across different teams, or segments can help in prioritizing resources or identify a gap in training or support. Alternatively, it may signify a best practice that can be uncovered.

Coupled with other metrics such as the sales cycle length or lead source will provide additional insight into which segments are closing deals faster or which source provides more wins. This information can then be further used to refine the sales strategy to provide additional focus on these and increase sales.

**Average Opportunity Age**

This metric shows the average time (usually in days) an opportunity stays in the pipeline. This is useful to know when identifying deals that have stalled. An opportunity that is in the pipeline above the average opportunity age should be investigated. This is to ensure that the prospect is being attended to and not forgotten or pushed aside by the salespeople. Keeping leads warm even if it is by an email or phone call can turn into an eventual sale.

Delays in progressing an opportunity may also be due to factors on the client's side. If so, it is important to understand why and update the CRM system accordingly. It might be prudent to drop the prospect, or file them for re-engagement at a later date.

**Average Sales Cycle Length**

The sales cycle length is the time it takes for an opportunity to move from being a lead to a win. A shorter sales cycle is desirable as it suggests an effective and optimized sales process. While this metric may vary between segments or between the industry sectors of your prospects, it should not vary too much ideally.

Comparing the average sales cycle length to the expected close dates in the funnel helps to keep opportunities on track. If there are delays in expected close dates, sales management should find out why during the pipeline management process. It may be an indication of a bottleneck in the process.

**Total Number of Open Opportunities**

Looking at the total number of open opportunities is a measure of workload. The more opportunities that are open, the more a salesperson has on his or her plate. This metric is monitored to ensure that your sales team has the resources to allocate to the opportunities.

If there are too many open opportunities, consider deploying additional salespeople from other teams, or prioritizing opportunities to ensure that the best leads do not turn cold. When there are too few open opportunities, then more leads should be generated to keep the pipeline flowing.

# Chapter 6: Generating Leads

Generating leads is also known as pipeline development, and it encompasses all the activities that builds the pipeline. Lead generation is about the identification and reaching out to potential customers, also known as prospects. Having a reliable and consistent way to generate leads is the first step in ensuring a healthy sales pipeline. Without any leads, there would be nothing to convert to wins!

More so than any other sales fix, having a consistent flow of leads into the pipeline will result in an increase in sales; the question then would be how many your salespeople can win. When there are insufficient leads going into the pipeline there are less opportunities that sales can afford to pass up on or afford to lose. Every other step in the process becomes a lot more crucial, and every loss is a huge blow to the possibility of meeting the budget. This is because the lead generation system can be scaled easily, but  increasing the win rate requires focusing on a number of interrelated factors that are more difficult to optimize.

Very commonly, there is a separation between sales and lead generation, which is usually a function of the marketing department. The common misconception is that since sales are the ones that need the leads, they should be the ones generating the leads.

## A Shift in the Buying Process

It is estimated at least 70% of customers reach out to vendors rather than having vendors reach out to them. It is estiamted by Propeller, a CRM company focusing on Google Apps, that 82% of customers viewed five or more pieces of content from the vendor they bought from before making a purchase, and also 70% of purchases made are to solve a specific problem.

This means that these prospects that enter the funnel are ready to buy, and Forrester Research has estimated that by the time they enter the sales pipeline the prospect would be more than halfway through their buying process.

This is due to the wealth of information being available online, and customers are able to do their own research online, learn about products or services, and even gather feedback from existing customers all before even speaking to a salesperson!

An online presence then is becoming more and more important. Lead generation then should build the relationship with the prospects before they are even identified.

## Outbound vs. Inbound Marketing

Outbound marketing is simply traditional advertising such as radio, television, print, telemarketing and such. Basically mass media is used to push the message with the aim of reaching the intended demographic in an interruptive manner, relying on a captive audience to make a pitch for attention.

Inbound marketing on the other hand aims to increase brand exposure and create authority in your organization's chosen field. The goal is to generate interest and get buyers to come to you instead of the other way around. With inbound marketing pull tactics are used in place of push tactics.

Common methods of inbound marketing are using blog or vlog posts, informational articles on websites, paid advertising, social media, and mobile apps to name a few. All these avenues of marketing require potential customers to come to your organization through their own free will; they have to go to a website, click a link, or search for your business or products online.

## Leads to Opportunities to Sales

So how many leads do you need? For the answer to that, we should look to the metrics and work backwards from the budget. By looking at the average size of deals won, we will now how many opportunities the sales team needs to win in order to achieve the budget. So if the sales budget is one million dollars and the average deal size is ten thousand dollars, then we can expect that the team would need 100 won opportunities to hit the budget target.

From that figure of 100 won opportunities we can then calculate how many closed sales we would need to get 100 wins, and from there figure out how many leads we need to get to the final figure of 100 won opportunities.

Using simple numbers as for an example, let's say the win rate is 10% and the close rate is 25%. That means to get 100 wins we would need 1,000 closed opportunities, and to get 1,000 closed opportunities, we would need 4,000 leads.

This final figure of 4,000 leads should then be scheduled to keep the number of open opportunities open per salesperson at a steady rate; this ensures that each individual salesperson is not overwhelmed and leads do not turn cold. That is why sales operations commonly breaks down the budget target by quarter, and have the sales team managers break down the targets further to an individual level.

Now back to the real world. A study by Hubspot, a Massachusetts CRM company, has showed that as the number of new leads generated per month increases, the less likely a business is to miss its revenue targets.

- 1-50 Leads - 72% polled did not achieve revenue target
- 51-100 Leads - 15% polled did not achieve revenue target
- 101-200 Leads - 4% polled did not achieve revenue target

So it is clear that the more leads you have the better.

# Chapter 7: Cleaning the Pipeline

The sales pipeline is a tool, and it is made up of a huge amount of data. Like any other tool, the sales pipeline needs regular upkeep and servicing as the data gets messy, out of date, or inaccurate. This is a way to ensure that the pipeline is performing at an optimal level, and everyone who uses the tool gets the most out of it.

While the accuracy of the information in the pipeline is directly proportional to the opportunities closed, sadly only 46% of salespeople trust that their pipeline is accurate. Having a good data policy, enforcing CRM usage, and regularly auditing the data are the first steps to building the trust in the system, and the integrity of the data.

## Use the CRM System

In the same way that there are standards for accounting, finance, and other departments to follow, salespeople must also be held to a certain standard which particularly revolves around the usage of the CRM system.

Setting up workflows and putting the usage of CRM as part of the process will encourage the sales people to regularly and consistently update and track their individual opportunities. Having a mobile enabled CRM will also help to drive adoption by giving salespeople the access they need without compromising on the mobility to do their job.

Since CRM systems are designed to work hand in hand with the sales pipeline, provide dashboards and produce in-depth analyses on the pipeline, it can provide a huge advantage if it is used correctly.

However, if it is not used or used only occasionally or selectively then the integrity of the system is compromised. In such situations, it would be unclear which pieces of information is updated, current, or reliable.

## Audit the Data Regularly

As the system is being used, data is being generated, and inaccurate or incomplete data can ruin the integrity of the system. Having a data policy when using the CRM to input data is just the first step. The data must be audited regularly to keep the integrity of the system.

Sales operations must regularly check the data for the most common culprits. These are:

- non uniform entries
- incomplete entries
- duplicate entries
- outdated entries

## Execute Regular Pipeline Reviews

Regular reviews of the pipeline keeps manages up to date on the performance of the salespeople to understand what is being done with each prospect that he or she is assigned to. Understanding the history of these opportunities, managers can then refer to the pipeline report or the CRM system to keep a record of this.

Reviews also serve to assess the quality of leads that are added to the funnel, and this is where management can have an influence on these opportunities; deciding which ones to prioritize and how the salespeople should focus their time.

## Engaged Opportunities Must be Entered

Simply put, there are two problems with the sales pipeline there is either too much irrelevant data in the pipeline, or the relevant data is not in the pipeline. The first usually happens when salespeople are overzealous in updating the pipeline with all their activities, and the second happens when the salespeople do not have the diligence or desire to update their pipeline.

A good practice is to insist that all prospects that are engaged must be entered into the pipeline, and only use it to track the leads and prospects that have been qualified. A company I used to work for would only review qualified deals, and only using the CRM system. They would also pay commission to salespeople only on deals marked as closed in the CRM system. While that might seem to be extreme to some people, it ensured that the CRM was one of the most useful tools I have ever used.

A good method to qualify a lead is to ensure that it has certain fields in the CRM system filled in. Most commonly the fields needed to qualify an opportunity are the prospect's budget, the name and details of the contacts within the prospect's organization, and an expected close date of the opportunity.

# Chapter 8: The Pipeline Review

Sales pipeline management is the organization and tracking of opportunities in the pipeline to track the progress of each opportunity. This is done by looking at trends, keeping an eye on the metrics, and ensuring a sufficient number of leads are being generated.

Reviewing the pipeline is most importantly done to assist the salespeople. It helps management understand how each salesperson is performing, if there are gaps in their training, and it helps managers identify what the salesperson should do next to move the opportunity in the pipeline.

## The Four Steps to Pipeline Review Progress

### Get an Update on the Opportunity

The first step of the review is to understand what has developed since the last review, or if this is the first time an opportunity is being reviewed, then it is important to understand the details of the opportunity. The update should include the following:

- What has happened so far?
- What are the next steps identified?
- What needs to happen to move the deal forward?
- What is the anticipated timeline?

## Identify Challenges or Obstacles

In the process of the update, challenges and obstacles will be evident. These will need to be addressed at some stage in order to move the deal forward and hopefully become a win eventually. Common obstacles to look out for are:

- Gaps in communication
- Gaps in knowledge
- The objections from the prospect
- The relationship between the salesperson and the prospect

## Decide on a Plan to Move the Deal Forward

After identifying the obstacles and challenges, there should be a clear idea of what needs to happen in order to move the deal forward in the pipeline, and if necessary, what additional resources need to be brought in. It should be clear if the salesperson is in control of the situation and is able to bring the opportunity to a win, or if additional support or coaching is needed.

In some cases a different product or solution may have to be proposed instead, which may delay the expected close dates. This may be preferable to pushing along with the current opportunity in the hopes of a deal being won. If a decision maker is not identified, there might be a need for your organization's management to provide support and ask for a meeting with the prospect's managers or decision makers.

In rare occasions it might be the most prudent thing to drop the prospect altogether, and just move on to another opportunity. In such an occasion, it should be the decision of sales management.

**Set a Timeline**

The last step of a review is to set a timeline for things to happen. When follow up calls or visits need to be made, when decision makers need to be identified, or when a product demonstration needs to be scheduled.

Alternatively, the timeline could be used to close gaps in performance or knowledge by attending training, or getting additional material. The end goal of this is to ensure that the salespeople have actionable items that they can perform between the present review and the next one.

Pipeline reviews are productive if used not for information gathering and deal updates, but for understanding the opportunities and working together with the salespeople to move them forward.

# Gaps in the Pipeline

Gaps or problems in the pipeline can surface when reviewing the pipeline. Most commonly, these gaps appear during reviews when we look for the commonly occurring obstacles or challenges that the salespeople face. Lack of presentations, templates, case studies or other materials is one example of such an issue.

Another way to find the gaps is to assess the pipeline by stage. These might be issues like bottlenecks, a high leakage rate, stale and stagnant opportunities, or any other number of things.

The key is to listen to the feedback of the salespeople, and correlate that with the metrics and insights from analyzing the pipeline.

# Chapter 9: After the Sale

After the ink is dry on the contract, the deal is closed and considered won. However, for the salesperson the job should not end here. This prospect is now a customer, but there is still an opportunity.

## Update the CRM

The CRM should be the central depositary of client information. Prospects should be entered when they become qualified leads, but once they sign the contracts, the engagement history, and the other details should also be updated.

This gives a good launching platform for the next engagement with the customer. It also communicates updates to the other departments like customer service, operations, and other departments who many interact with the customer. Updating the CRM ensures that these other departments are brought up to date quickly, and ensures the level of service they provide will maintain the standard that has been set by sales.

## Follow Up with the Customer

A weak follow up and poor communication can cost your business a customer, but a strong follow up can build loyalty with the customer and uncover more opportunities. After an opportunity is closed, it is a good practice to schedule a follow up.

This is not only to ensure the customer is satisfied, and build on the relationship that has been built. Additionally, this is an opportunity for the salesperson to:

1. Uncover up-selling or cross-selling opportunities
2. Ask for referrals to other leads

The above can only happen if the customer has a positive experience with your organization, and the sales pipeline built on a solid foundation of a well thought out sales process is the first step towards that.

**Up-selling and Cross-selling**

Up-selling and cross-selling is a bid to get an increase on the bottom line of the sale. It is important that the up-selling or cross-selling suggestion is made with the customer's needs and preferences in mind. The idea is not to present a large number of options to the customer but instead selectively offer additional products and services.

These offers presented have to make sense to the customer, in the same way McDonald's tries to get you to super-size a meal; they are phrasing their offering of additional food for a small increase in price.

**Ask for referrals to other leads**

After closing an opportunity, the easiest way to generate more leads is to ask for them. Your customers will very likely know others in their industry who would benefit from your product or service offerings.

Being introduced also immediately pre-qualifies the lead and makes it easier to build trust with the new prospect. This is probably the best type of leads to get, and is an easy way to grow the pipeline and generate more sales. Nielsen, a global marketing research firm, has found that referrals are 4 times more likely to buy because of the inherent trust of a friend being transferred to the salesperson.

While many salespeople are reluctant to ask for materials, making this a part of closing the sales process and coaching them to do this will help to build the business. After all, 91% of customers are willing to give referrals according to Propeller, a CRM company focusing on Google apps. However, in the same study it was found that only 11% of salespeople actually asked for referrals. This was corroborated by another research done by Texas Tech University, where their figures were 83% and 29% respectively.

# Chapter 10: Technology and the Pipeline

## Automating the Pipeline

As the concept of sales pipelines evolve along with sales processes, it can get more and more complex. Sales cycles are getting longer, increasing by about 20% according to a 2017 study by AgileCRM, a SaaS CRM company.

In a Forbes 2016 article it was found that sales teams increase their revenue, and are able to meet targets 20% higher than the previous year when automation was used to assist sales. This is mainly because low value and time consuming tasks are usually the first ones to be automated; this allows salespeople more time in the fields to sell.

Automation then will help to alleviate some of the workload and speed up processes. Once automation has been introduced to the pipeline, leads and opportunities will not be overlooked or left to go stale and cold. Salespeople are able to move from being reactive to being proactive in reaching out to leads and prospects.

According to a 2016 blogpost by Salesforce, a leading CRM provider, at least 40% of sales tasks can be automated. This is expected to be increased to 50% in the near future. Here are some of the elements of the pipeline that are commonly automated:

- Lead Qualification

- Prospect Allocation
- Pipeline Tracking
- Alerts and Follow Ups
- Quotations, Proposals, and Order Management

## Lead Qualifiaction

Qualifying leads is automated by understanding the behavior of the lead, along with a scoring system. Actions that the prospect takes, such as visiting your company's website or sending an email can be scored as being a more interested customer. Conversely, not opening an email from your organization, having a low "stick rate" on the website and other behaviors may result in a customer being tagged as less interested.

This is not completely fool proof, but with enough robustness built into the scoring system it is possible to account for minor anomalies and discrepancies.

## Prospect Allocation

Allocating prospects to salespeople is an art and requires many factors to be considered. From the capability and experience of the salespeople, to the industries that he or she has experience with, to how many opportunities that each salesperson has open must be considered.

Automating prospect allocation makes this decision for you by using a set of predefined rules.

## Pipeline Tracking

It is a best practice to have a checklist for each stage of the sales pipeline. This ensures that the salesperson follows the sales process at large, and the prospect is engaged accordingly. Information is gathered from or presented to the prospect as necessary to move towards the close.

Automating the tracking of the pipeline ensures that salespeople do not skip a step in their eagerness to move a sales forward.

## Alerts and Follow Ups

On an individual level, automation can be used to lighten the workload of the salespeople. Tracking the length of time that each opportunity spends in the current stage of the pipeline, prompts can be triggered to remind the salesperson to follow up.

Once certain activities have taken place, prompts can be made to move the opportunity to the next stage of the sales pipeline. This prevents inconsistencies in the data, and keeps the pipeline and other CRM data as updated as possible.

An example is to have an automated opening email sent to the prospect as soon as the lead is assigned and accepted by the salesperson. This email is usually customized slightly by individual salespeople but contains the best practice elements identified by sales operations.

Similar emails could also be triggered at various points of the sales process, by sending product demonstration videos, product catalogues, or a specific case study. These emails to the prospect help drive the prospect to the next stage of the pipeline and eventually to a win.

Such automation of scheduling and emails helps to keep accounts covered on a regular cadence, and keeps the salespeople visible to the prospects.

**Quotations, Proposals, and Order Management**

Time savings from automation can also be realized in preparing sales documents. Quotations, proposals, and orders are commonly handled by salespeople and can be time consuming. Having these documents on a template and automated frees up the time of.

# Going Mobile

Aside from automation, being mobile is another huge game changer. With systems being cloud based, this means that they are available on mobile devices. Remember that pipeline management is part of most CRM systems.

Therefore being mobile is a huge increase in productivity; 15% to be exact according to Salesforce. Salespeople will have access to leads, logs, customer history, and sales data at any time, which allows them to have a more value based discussion when out in the field.

Purchase times have shown to be reduced, and that has led to increased profits for businesses that employ mobile applications. Research from Tapp.com has shown that mobile CRM increases the rate at salespeople achieve their targets with 65% of mobile CRM users meeting their quotas as compared to 22% where there was no mobile CRM.

# Conclusion

Thank you for taking the time to read this book!

I hope that you have gained an understanding of how a well managed sales pipeline can benefit your sales team. If you enjoyed this book, please take the time to leave me a review on Amazon. I appreciate your honest feedback, and it really helps me to continue producing high quality books.